Marley & Me

JOHN GROGAN

Level 2

Retold by Anne Collins
Series Editors: Andy Hopkins and Jocelyn Potter

Pearson Education Limited
Edinburgh Gate, Harlow,
Essex CM20 2JE, England
and Associated Companies throughout the world.

ISBN: 978-1-4082-6376-1

This edition first published by Pearson Education Ltd 2012

5 7 9 10 8 6

Set in 11/14pt Bembo
Printed in China
SWTC/05

Penguin Books Ltd a Penguin Random House company

The publisher would like to thank the following for their kind permission
to reproduce their photographs:

John Grogan: 5, 10, 16, 24, 28

Every effort has been made to trace the copyright holders and we apologise in advance
for any unintentional omissions. We would be pleased to insert the appropriate
acknowledgement in any subsequent edition of this publication.

For a complete list of the titles available in the Penguin Readers series please go to
www.penguinreaders.com. Alternatively, write to your local Pearson Longman office
or to: Penguin Readers Marketing Department, Pearson Education,
Edinburgh Gate, Harlow, Essex CM20 2JE, England.

Contents

		page
Introduction		iv
Chapter 1	The New Puppy	1
Chapter 2	Life with Marley	5
Chapter 3	The Obedience Class	8
Chapter 4	Changes at Home	13
Chapter 5	Difficult Days	17
Chapter 6	Marley Makes a Movie	21
Chapter 7	The World's Worst Dog	25
Chapter 8	We Move North	29
Chapter 9	Marley Gets Older	31
Chapter 10	A Great Dog	35
Activities		39

Introduction

A dog isn't interested in fast cars or big houses or expensive clothes.
Give a dog your love, and he will give you his.

Marley and Me is about a dog, but it is also about a family and their love for their dog, Marley. John Grogan and his wife, Jenny, are young and in love. They have good jobs on newspapers. Then, one day, they go out and buy a puppy. From that day, their lives are never the same again.

Marley is not an easy dog. He isn't obedient and he doesn't listen. He pushes things off tables with his strong, heavy tail, and he eats everything—flowers, pens, and bottle tops. He goes crazy in thunderstorms, and he breaks things in the home.

But life with Marley is never boring. Many funny things happen when he is there. And, most important, he brings John and Jenny a lot of love. He helps them understand the important things in life.

The story follows Marley's life from a puppy to an old dog. In that time, we see many changes, not only in Marley but in the family, too. At the start, John and Jenny are living in a busy city in Florida. Thirteen years later, they have three children and are living a quieter life in Pennsylvania.

John Grogan worked on newspapers for more than twenty-five years. When he wrote funny stories about Marley, readers wrote to him about their love for their dogs—and their problems, too. Later, John made his stories into a book, *Marley & Me*. Then, in 2009, a film company made a movie of the book, with Jennifer Aniston and Owen Wilson. Now people around the world are enjoying the story of "the world's worst dog." You can find out more about John Grogan—and his dogs—on www.johngroganbooks.com.

Chapter 1 The New Puppy

My name is John Grogan and I love dogs. When I was ten years old, my father gave me my first dog. I called him Shaun.

Shaun was my best friend. He went everywhere with me and he was very obedient. When I called him, he came to me. He played with me and he walked next to me without a leash. In the car, he sat next to me quietly.

After many years, Shaun died. He was fourteen years old. By that time, I wasn't a boy; I was a man. I had my first job.

Shaun was a great dog. I wanted to get another dog, but it had to be as wonderful as Shaun.

♦

Some years later, I moved to Florida and married Jenny. Jenny and I had jobs with newspapers. We were very happy. We were young and in love, and life was wonderful.

One day, I bought a plant for Jenny. It was very large, with beautiful white flowers. Jenny loved it—maybe too much. Every day, she gave it water. In the end, the plant got sick and died.

Some days later, I woke up early. Jenny wasn't in bed. I found her at the table with a newspaper. She had a red pen in her hand.

"Jenny," I said, "what are you doing?"

She showed me the newspaper. It was open at a page of ads.

"Look at this, John," she said.

I saw an ad with a big red line under it:

Beautiful Labrador* puppies. Five weeks old.

"I can't forget about that plant," Jenny said. "Why couldn't

---

* Labrador: a kind of large dog. Labradors are usually black, yellow, or dark brown, and are good pets.

I look after a plant? I only had to give it water, but I killed it." She looked sad, but then she smiled. "I can't look after a plant, but maybe I can look after a dog. And later, maybe I'll be ready for a baby."

I thought about that. Jenny and I wanted to have children one day, but we loved dogs, too. Our little house was a good place for a dog. We lived near a park and near a beach. And the house had a big yard with lots of trees.

"OK," I said. I put my arms around Jenny. "Let's get a dog."

So some days later, we drove to the address in the ad. The house was in the middle of some woods. A woman came to the door and there was a beautiful yellow Labrador with her.

"I'm Lori," said the woman. "And this is Lily. She's the puppies' mother."

"Where's the father?" I asked.

"Oh," said Lori. "Sammy Boy? He's—er—around here somewhere." Then she said quickly, "Do you want to see the puppies?"

Lori took us into a room behind the kitchen. There were a lot of newspapers on the floor, and a large box by the wall. In the box were nine yellow puppies.

"Oh!" cried Jenny. "Aren't they beautiful?"

We sat on the floor with the puppies. One little puppy really liked us. He climbed up our shirts and looked into our eyes.

"The puppies are $375 each," said Lori. "But you can have that puppy for $350."

I stood up and turned away from the puppies. Then I turned back quickly and shouted loudly. The other puppies ran away. But the little puppy ran to me and climbed over my shoes.

"That's our puppy," Jenny laughed.

I held him in front of my face. I looked at him and he looked at me. He had very large brown eyes. I gave him to

Jenny, and she held him, too.

"I think he likes us," I said.

We paid Lori for him.

"Come back for him in three weeks," she said. "He'll be eight weeks old, so you can take him then."

We thanked Lori and said goodbye. On our way to the car, I put my arm around Jenny.

"Isn't it wonderful?" I said. "We got our dog."

"Yes," she said. "I can't wait to bring him home."

Suddenly, we heard a loud noise in the woods. Something ran out of the trees—something large and yellow. It was a big Labrador. But this dog was very different from Lily. This dog was wild and dirty. It had a crazy look in its eyes. It ran quickly past us, and around the back of the house.

"I think," I said slowly, "that's Dad."

♦

Jenny and I tried to think of a name for our puppy, but each of us liked different names.

One morning, we heard a song by Bob Marley, the Jamaican singer, on the radio. Bob Marley was dead, but people played his music everywhere in Florida. Jenny and I liked his music, too.

Suddenly, at the same time, we shouted, "Marley!"

"That's it!" I cried. "That's his name. Marley!" Jenny smiled.

Some days later, Jenny's sister called her from Boston.

"We're visiting Disney World next week with the children," she said. "Would you like to come with us?"

Jenny wanted to go to Disney World very much. "But I won't be here when Marley comes home," she said.

"That's OK," I said. "I'll go and get Marley."

A week later, Jenny left for Orlando. That evening after work, I drove to Lori's house. Marley was a very large puppy now.

"He eats a lot," said Lori.

"Are you ready for your new home, Marley?" I said. I used his name for the first time and it felt right.

Marley sat next to me in the car. He tried to climb on me, but each time, he fell back on the floor. In the end, he climbed up and sat on me. He wagged his tail happily.

When we got home, I took off his leash. Marley began to sniff. He went around the house and sniffed everything. Then he sat back and looked at me with his large brown eyes.

I could read Marley's thoughts: *This place is great. But where are my brothers and sisters?*

I took Marley to the garage, next to the house. It was a warm, dry room.

"Marley," I said. "This is your room now."

I put some newspapers down on the floor. I put some playthings down, too. Then I put some water in a bowl and made a bed from a large box.

"You're going to sleep here," I said. I put Marley into the box. He looked sadly up at me. I went back into the house and closed the door. I stood and listened. I could hear nothing. Then I heard a cry—and then another cry. The cries got louder and louder.

When I opened the door again, Marley stopped crying. I petted him for some time. Then I left again and closed the door. Marley started to cry again.

I was very tired, so I went to my bedroom. My bedroom wasn't near the garage, but I could hear Marley's cries. I felt sorry for him. His family wasn't there.

After I got into bed, I listened to Marley's cries for half an hour. Then I got up and went back to the garage. Marley stopped crying and wagged his tail. I carried his box into my bedroom and put it on the floor next to my bed. Then I got into bed and put my hand down into the box.

Some minutes later, Marley was asleep. I slept, too.

Marley tried to understand us.

Chapter 2 Life with Marley

For the next three days, I played with Marley. I lay on the floor and he climbed on me. He followed me everywhere, and he tried to chew on everything.

When Jenny came back from Disney World, she played with Marley, too. She held him and petted him. She got up in the night and took him outside. Most of all, she gave him food. Marley ate three large bowls of puppy food every day. He got bigger all the time. His head and his paws were very large, and his tail was thick and heavy. When he wagged his tail, he pushed everything onto the floor—magazines and glasses, and photos.

Marley loved to grab things and hold them in his mouth. He

grabbed things from the floor and from the dining-room table. He grabbed shoes, pens, bottle tops, and many other things.

"All right, what have you got this time?" I asked. When I opened his mouth, I always found something new inside.

Every morning, I took Marley for a walk on the beach. Then I put him in the garage with a bowl of water and some playthings. After that, I went to work. I always said, "Be a good boy, Marley!" Jenny came home at lunchtime and gave him food.

In the evenings, we took Marley down to the beach again. But our walks weren't easy. Marley ran in front of us and pulled on his leash. We pulled him back, then he pulled us again. He went this way and that way, and he sniffed everything.

We tried to teach Marley, "Come! Stay! Sit! Down! No!" But he didn't listen to us. He wasn't obedient. He was like an excited child. But every day he got bigger and stronger.

"I killed the plant, but I'm good with Marley," Jenny said happily.

One day, Jenny invited a friend to our house. Her friend brought her old dog, Buddy, with her. Buddy and Marley ran and played. Then they were tired, so they lay down in the yard.

Some days later, Jenny was with Marley when she said, "Come and look at this, John!"

I looked, and I saw something small and black in Marley's fur.

"Oh, no!" I said. "Marley has fleas."

They were on his paws, inside his ears, and under his tail.

"Buddy had fleas and he gave them to Marley," said Jenny angrily.

She ran out and got into her car. Half an hour later, she came back with bags of chemicals. First, she washed Marley's fur with the chemicals. Then she put him in the garage and cleaned the house carefully. I cleaned the yard. Every day after that, we looked in Marley's fur, but we couldn't see any more fleas.

♦

Some weeks later, Jenny said, "John, I'm going to have a baby!"

"That's wonderful," I said. I was very happy. We were ready for a baby now.

Then Jenny said, "But will those chemicals be a problem?"

"What chemicals?" I asked. "What do you mean?"

"Don't you remember? I used very strong chemicals when Marley had fleas. They can't be good for a baby," she said.

She talked to her doctor about the chemicals.

"It's all right, Jenny," he said. "Everything will be OK."

Jenny got up early every day and took Marley for a walk. She ate lots of fruits and vegetables. After ten weeks, she and I saw the doctor again.

"Would you like to see your baby?" he asked.

"Yes, please," we said. We felt very excited.

The doctor took us into a room at the back and Jenny lay down. He moved something over Jenny. On a machine next to him, we could see something like a small gray bag. But we couldn't see a baby inside.

"Is there anything in there?" asked Jenny.

After a time, the doctor said quietly, "I'm very sorry, Jenny. Your baby's dead."

I felt sick. I sat and held Jenny's hand. We didn't say anything for a long time. When the doctor left, I put my arms around my wife. Later, I took her home. She was very quiet in the car. Her eyes were red, but she didn't cry.

Back home, Jenny went into the dining-room and sat down quietly on a chair. I got Marley from the garage. He was very excited. He jumped up and wagged his tail. He wanted to play.

"Not today, Marley," I said sadly.

Marley ran into the yard. He came back into the house and drank water from his bowl. Then he ran into the dining-room and I followed him. But at the door of the dining-room, I stopped.

I saw a wonderful thing. Marley stood quietly in front of Jenny with his tail between his legs. He put his big head on her legs. He looked at her with his large eyes and made small cries.

"Marley understands," I thought.

Jenny petted his head and put her face in his fur. Then, suddenly, she began to cry. I went to them and put my arms around them. The three of us stayed there for a long time— Jenny, Marley, and me.

Chapter 3   The Obedience Class

When Marley was six months old, Dr. Jay, the animal doctor, told us about an obedience class.

We loved Marley very much, but he wasn't an obedient dog. Every day he got bigger and stronger, and he didn't listen to us. He jumped up on us. He grabbed things in the house and chewed them. When I bought flowers for Jenny, Marley ate them.

We met the teacher of the obedience class. She had a cold face and she didn't smile.

"There are no bad dogs," she said, "but there are some very weak *people*."

The class was every Tuesday evening. We put Marley into the car and drove to the first class. When Marley saw the other dogs, he got very excited. A party! He jumped out of the car. I ran after him, but I couldn't catch him. Marley sniffed every dog before I caught his leash.

"Take that dog back to his place in the line," said the teacher. "Who is going to be his boss—you or your wife?"

"I am," I said.

"Me, too," said Jenny.

"No," said the teacher. "A dog can only have *one* boss."

"OK," said Jenny. "I'll do it."

The other dogs sat quietly in a line. Jenny took Marley to his place. I stood and watched.

Suddenly, Marley saw another dog at the end of the line. That dog looked interesting! He started to pull Jenny. She tried to stop him, but she couldn't. Marley was stronger than Jenny, so he pulled her to the other dog. Then he sniffed around it.

"That dog thinks *he's* the boss," said the teacher coldly.

She started to teach the class "Sit!" and "Down!".

"Sit!" Jenny told Marley. But Marley didn't want to sit. He jumped up and put his paws on Jenny.

After the class, the teacher said, "You have to be strong with that animal. You're the boss. Show him that."

When we got home, Jenny said, "*You* can take Marley to the class next week."

The next Tuesday, Marley and I went back to the class. Jenny stayed at home. In the car, I said to Marley, "*I'm* the boss! You're not the boss—*I'm* the boss! Do you understand?" But Marley only looked at me and wagged his tail. Then he tried to chew my hands.

In this lesson, the dogs had to walk quietly next to us. It was a very important lesson for Marley. When he went for a walk with Jenny and me, he always pulled us. The teacher gave us chains.

"Put the chain over your dog's head," she said. "When he pulls you, pull him back with it. It will hurt him, so he'll stop pulling."

I tried to put the chain over Marley's head but Marley, of course, got very excited. A new game! He grabbed the chain with his teeth. I tried again, but each time, Marley grabbed it.

In the end, I got the chain over Marley's head and started to walk with him. When Marley pulled in front of me, I pulled him back with the chain. But then he pulled away again.

Marley loved to chew on his leash.

"Here," said the teacher. "I'll show you."

She took Marley's leash and started to walk with him. Marley pulled the chain, and the teacher pulled him back. But then Marley pulled the chain again. This new game was great!

Then Marley saw me. He started to run to me and he pulled the teacher after him. Marley was bigger and stronger than the teacher, so she couldn't stop him. She was very angry.

After class, the teacher said, "Your dog isn't ready for this class. He's too young. You can bring him back in six or eight months."

"Are you telling us that we have to leave the class?" I said.

"That's right," she said. "You have to leave."

♦

Because Marley couldn't go back to the class, I started to teach him at home. But it was difficult. Marley wasn't a fast learner.

We had another problem with Marley. In Florida, there were often thunderstorms. Marley was afraid of loud noises. He went crazy in a storm. He broke things and made everything dirty.

After each storm, Marley quickly forgot about it. He was happy again and wanted to play. But in the next storm, the same thing happened. He was afraid, so he went crazy again.

We talked to Dr. Jay about the problem. Dr. Jay was young and he understood dogs very well.

"What can we do?" we asked. "When Marley gets crazy, he breaks things. One day, he'll get hurt in a storm."

"Marley is seven months old," said Dr. Jay. "I'll neuter him. Then he won't get so excited. He'll be a quieter, happier dog."

I thought about that. "Oh," I said. "I don't really know … "

"Yes!" said Jenny. "That's a great idea!"

"Bring Marley here on your way to work," said Dr. Jay. "It doesn't take long. He'll be ready by the afternoon. You can get him again on your way home."

A week later, we took Marley to Dr. Jay. Marley ran from the house and jumped into the car. He was very happy. He loved to go out with Jenny and me—his two best friends.

Jenny drove and I sat next to her with Marley. He pushed at the window with his nose. He wanted to sniff outside the car. I opened the window and Marley put his nose outside.

"I feel sorry for Marley," I said to Jenny. Then I looked at him. His front paws were out of the window.

"John," said Jenny, "what's Marley doing? Please be careful."

"He's fine," I said. "He only wants to put his head outside."

Marley put his head out of the window. Then suddenly, he pushed his front legs out, too. He tried to jump down on the road. But the road was very busy with cars.

"John!" shouted Jenny. "Hold him!"

Jenny tried to stop the car, but she couldn't. The other cars drove around us very fast. It was very dangerous. Now Marley's front paws were down on the road. He ran next to the car. I grabbed him by his tail and Jenny stopped the car.

"Now what?" I shouted.

I couldn't pull Marley back into the car. I couldn't open the door. I couldn't get my other arm out. And there were cars all around us. The other drivers looked at us angrily.

Jenny opened her door and got out of the car. She ran around it and grabbed Marley. I opened my door and got out, too. In the end, we got Marley back into the car.

When we got to Dr. Jay's, I took Marley inside. He sniffed everywhere, then he pushed over a table with magazines on it.

I gave Marley's leash to Dr. Jay.

"Please neuter him as quickly as possible," I said. "Please."

That evening, when I took Marley home, I saw a change in him. He wasn't excited and crazy. He moved quietly and slowly.

"Good," I thought.

Chapter 4 Changes at Home

Jenny and I worked hard at our jobs. We also worked hard at home. So one evening I said, "Let's go on vacation, Jenny."

The next day, I bought two airplane tickets. They were for a three-week vacation in Ireland.

"What are we going to do about Marley?" asked Jenny.

"We can leave him in the house," I said. "Somebody can stay here with him."

"Marley is a difficult dog," said Jenny. "That person will have to be kind but also strong. He or she will have to be his boss."

"I know," I said. Then I had an idea. "Kathy loves animals."

Kathy worked in my office. The next day, I asked her and she said yes. Before she arrived, I wrote some notes for her about Marley. There were six pages of notes. I showed them to Jenny.

"Did I forget anything?" I asked.

Jenny read the notes, then she said, "You can't tell Kathy all that. She won't want to stay with Marley."

But when Kathy read the notes, she smiled. "Marley and I will be fine," she said. "Have a great vacation."

♦

Jenny and I had a wonderful vacation in Ireland. The weather was fine and warm. We drove on small country roads and walked by the ocean. At night, we stayed in the houses of Irish families. We forgot about our jobs in Florida.

When we arrived home, Marley ran outside to us. Kathy stood at the door. She looked very tired. Her bag was next to her.

"I'm sorry," she said, "but Marley broke a lot of things in the house. He wasn't obedient and he didn't listen to me."

We thanked Kathy, but she wanted to leave very quickly.

I turned to Marley. "All right, Marley," I said. "Tomorrow you're going to learn about obedience."

The next morning, Jenny and I went back to work. But first, I put the chain around Marley's neck and took him for a walk. Marley started to pull me.

"Sit, Marley!" I said. Marley sat.

"OK, let's try that again," I said.

We started to walk and Marley pulled me again. I made the chain very short and pulled him back. It hurt him, but it was the only way. In the end, he learned his lesson. He walked next to me and didn't pull me.

I felt very happy. "Good, Marley," I said. "*I'm* the boss."

Some days later, Jenny called me at the office.

"John," she said. "I went to see the doctor. I'm going to have a baby."

♦

This time, Jenny and I were very careful and we put away every chemical in the house. Jenny looked well. She got up early each morning and took Marley for a walk by the ocean. When we went to the doctor, we saw our baby on the machine.

But I didn't forget about Marley. I worked with him every day. Marley was more obedient now, but he didn't listen to me all the time. He came when I called him—sometimes.

In our yard we had a fruit tree. Marley loved eating fruit, but it went through him quickly. His poop was everywhere in the yard. He ate a lot of other things, too. These went through him and came out in his poop—toys, pens, and bottle tops.

I bought Jenny a beautiful chain for her birthday. She loved it and she put it around her neck. But some hours later she cried, "My chain! Where is it? Maybe I didn't put it on right."

"We didn't go outside," I said. "So it's here in the house."

We looked in every room, but we couldn't find the chain.

Suddenly Jenny said, "What's that in Marley's mouth?"

I saw the end of a thin chain. "Oh, no!" I cried. "OK, Marley, it's all right. Come here now. Please give us the chain."

But Marley only looked at us. Suddenly, he threw his head back.

"He's eating the chain!" cried Jenny.

I opened his mouth and pushed my hand down. But I couldn't find the chain.

"We'll have to wait," I said. "The chain will go through Marley and come out in his poop."

I gave Marley lots of fruit. We waited for three days. I followed Marley everywhere. When he pooped, I looked for the chain. But it wasn't there.

On the fourth day, I found it. After I washed it, it was very clean. It had a beautiful shine.

"That's wonderful," Jenny said. "It shines better than before."

Jenny wore that chain for years. When I saw it, I always thought of Marley.

♦

Our son was born in St. Mary's Hospital in Palm Beach. We called him Patrick, an Irish name.

"Things are going to change at home for Marley now," said Jenny. "Maybe he won't like the changes."

I brought Jenny and Patrick home from the hospital. Patrick was asleep and we put him on our bed. Then we went to the garage and brought Marley into the house. He followed Jenny into the bedroom, but he didn't see Patrick on the bed.

Then Patrick made a small noise and Marley's ears went up.
Where did that noise come from?

Patrick made another noise. Marley held up a paw, and Jenny and I watched him.

"What's Marley going to do?" I thought.

Marley jumped up onto the bed. I pulled him back quickly

15

and held him. Patrick's eyes were very wide. But Marley didn't want to hurt Patrick. He sniffed all around him.

Now Marley had a new best friend. When he was near Patrick, he wasn't wild and crazy. At night, he slept under Patrick's bed.

Six months later, Patrick started to move around. Marley lay on the floor and Patrick climbed over him. Sometimes Patrick pulled Marley's fur. But Marley lay quietly and didn't move.

We were parents now and we were happy. We had our wonderful baby. We had our dog. We had our house by the ocean. Life was good.

Marley wasn't an obedient dog, but he was always happy.

Then, when Patrick was nine months old, Jenny said, "I'm going to have another baby."

Chapter 5 Difficult Days

Sometimes, bad things happened in our street.

One night, in October, Jenny and I were in bed. Marley lay on the floor next to me. Suddenly, I heard a cry—the cry of a girl. It came from the street outside.

I felt afraid, but I jumped out of bed. "Come with me, Marley," I said.

"Please, John, don't go out there," said Jenny.

"Call the police," I said. "I'll be careful."

I held Marley by the end of his chain. The girl cried again. We went outside, and a man ran away down the street. Two young men ran to me.

"Go and stay with the girl," they shouted. "Help her. We're going after the man."

I ran to the girl. She was my neighbor's daughter, Lisa. She was seventeen years old. Her shirt was red and wet.

"What happened?" I asked.

"I was in my car," she said. "A man got in and put his hand over my mouth. He said, 'Don't make a noise!' But I did, and he cut me with his knife."

I held Lisa in my arms. "It's going to be all right," I said. But I didn't really think that. Lisa's face was gray, and she was very weak.

I looked at Marley. He stood and looked down the street. He looked strong and ready for a fight. Nobody could get past him.

Some minutes later the police arrived, with doctors, and they took Lisa away. A policeman asked me questions. Then I went home with Marley.

Jenny met us at the door.

"Marley was a different dog tonight," I said. "Nothing can hurt us when he's with us." I looked at Marley. "You did well tonight, " I said.

Lisa didn't die. She got well again. But I never forgot that night.

♦

One night, when Jenny and I were in bed, she said, "John, I think the baby is coming. Please call the doctor."

"Something's wrong," I thought. "It's too early for the baby."

I took Jenny to the hospital.

"Your baby is too small," the doctor said to her. "We have to stop him coming out. You'll have to stay in the hospital."

Jenny was in the hospital for twelve days. I stayed at home with Patrick and Marley. I did the housework. I cooked and washed clothes. In the evenings, I was very tired.

Marley sat and looked at me sadly. I could read his thoughts.

I don't understand. Why doesn't John want to play with me? Why doesn't he take me for walks? And where's Jenny?

I didn't do things at home very well. I left the bathroom door open all the time. Marley loved to go into the bathroom, and to drink water from the shower.

One day, I took Patrick on a visit to the hospital.

"What did you do to Patrick?" Jenny asked.

"What do you mean?" I asked. "He's fine."

"Look at him," said Jenny.

I looked. His arms were in the legs of his baby clothes!

Jenny called my aunt Anita. She also lived in Florida, but in a different town.

"Please can you look after John and Patrick," she said.

Two days later, Aunt Anita arrived. She did the housework and everything at home was fine again.

♦

When Jenny came home, she had to stay in bed all day. This was a very difficult time for her. She couldn't cook or go for

18

a walk. Worst of all, she couldn't hold Patrick.

Marley brought his playthings into the bedroom and lay on the floor next to Jenny. He stayed there day and night.

Aunt Anita had to go home to her husband. So I had to look after the house again.

Then, one day, when the doctor visited Jenny, he said, "You can get up now. The baby is bigger."

Jenny was very happy. She got up and played with Patrick and Marley. She started to do the housework.

The next day, we went to a Greek restaurant for lunch. But suddenly, the baby started to come, so I took Jenny to the hospital. Then everything happened very quickly. One hour later, I held my beautiful new son in my arms.

♦

Jenny and I had two sons now, Patrick and Conor. One was seventeen months old, and one was a baby. We were very happy with our sons, but we were tired all the time. The babies woke us every night. We couldn't sleep for more than two hours.

Conor had problems with Jenny's milk. After he drank, he was sick. So Jenny was very sad.

"What's wrong with me?" she said. "Conor doesn't like my milk. Maybe I'm not a good mom."

She started to get angry quickly. She didn't get angry with Patrick and Conor, but she was often angry with Marley and me.

Marley could do nothing right. I bought a plant and planted it in the yard. The next day, Marley pulled it out and ate it. Then he broke a door in the house. He went crazy when there was a thunderstorm.

One day when I got home from work, I found Marley with Jenny. Jenny was very, very angry.

"Why do you break everything?" she shouted. "You're a

19

very bad dog." Marley stood with his head down, and she hit him again and again.

I went and grabbed Jenny's arms.

"Hey! Hey! Hey!" I shouted. "Stop. Stop!"

I looked into Jenny's face, but the look in her eyes was new to me. Her face was the face of a stranger.

"Get him out of here," she said. "Get him out of here now."

I opened the front door and Marley ran outside. When I turned back for his leash, Jenny said, "You have to find Marley a new home."

She couldn't mean it. She loved this dog. I walked out of the door. Marley ran and jumped around. He wasn't hurt.

I took Marley into the street and said, "Sit!" He sat. I put his chain over his head with the leash. Then I took him for a very long walk. When we got home, Marley was very tired.

I took off Marley's leash and he ran to his bowl. The water went everywhere on the floor. I cleaned it.

Jenny sat in a chair with Patrick and Conor. When I walked past her, she said quietly, "I want that dog to leave."

♦

I felt very sad. Marley was my friend and I loved him. I didn't want to find a new home for him. But I also had a wife and two small children. I had to think about them.

I talked to my friends and neighbors about Marley.

"Do you want a Labrador?" I asked. But nobody did.

I looked in the newspapers. They were full of ads from people with dogs, and a lot of the ads were for Labradors.

"These people paid a lot of money for their dogs," I thought. "But now they're looking for new homes for them. Maybe Labradors are too difficult—too big and strong."

Marley wasn't an easy dog. He wasn't obedient and he broke things. But we brought him to our home when he was a puppy. He loved us and we loved him. He was *our* dog.

I took Marley back to the obedience class. A different teacher was there now. This time, things went better. I said "Sit!" and Marley sat. I put the chain around his neck and he walked quietly next to me. I said "Stay!" and he stayed. I walked away from him, but he didn't move. Then I turned and said, "Come!" Marley ran quickly to me.

"Good boy, Marley," I said. "Good, good, good boy!"

At the end of the eight weeks, the teacher gave me a paper. It said, "Marley did well in the obedience class."

I was very happy. On the way home, I sang.

After this, a wonderful thing happened. Jenny got better. She stopped being sad, and was strong and happy. She was a good mother to Patrick and Conor, and she was kind to Marley again. She danced around the room with him. Sometimes at night, when he was quiet, she lay on the floor with him, her head on his neck.

"Jenny's here with us again," I thought. "That's great!"

Chapter 6 Marley Makes a Movie

Jenny's friend Colleen worked for a film company. One day, Colleen called Jenny.

"My company is making a film about a family in Florida," she said. "They want pictures of a family home. Can I come and take some pictures of your house?"

Colleen came and took photos of our home and the children—and of Marley, too. She showed them to her boss, Bob Gosse.

Some days later, Jenny called me at work.

"Bob Gosse is making a movie about a family with a dog," she said excitedly. "So he's looking for a dog—a big, family dog. He saw Colleen's photos and he's interested in Marley."

"Really?" I said. "You mean … Marley? *Our* Marley?"

The next day, Colleen came to our house and took Marley to her boss. Two hours later, she brought him back again.

"Marley was great," she said. "Everybody loved him."

Some days later, the company started filming.

"Bring Marley to the Gulfstream Hotel at nine o'clock," Bob Gosse told us.

We put the children and Marley into the car and drove to the hotel. A lot of people stood outside. The police were there, too. One of the policemen looked inside the car. He saw Jenny, two small children, and a large dog.

"You can't come this way," he said. "You have to turn back."

"But we're with the film company," I said. "Our dog is in the movie."

"Really?" the police officer said. Then he looked at a paper in his hand. "You have the dog?" Marley's name was on the paper.

"I have the dog," I said. "Marley the Dog."

"Oh," said the policeman. He turned to another policeman and shouted, "He has the dog. Marley the Dog!" Then he turned to us again. "You can come in," he said.

I felt very important. Marley was famous!

The cameramen started to film Marley. But Marley wasn't obedient. He ran and jumped. He chewed through his leash.

"Cut! Cut! Cut!" shouted Bob Gosse.

At the end of the day, we took Marley home.

"Marley," I said sadly, "you're not going to be famous."

But the next day, the film company called again.

"Please bring Marley back here," they said.

When we got back to the hotel, Bob Gosse said, "On film, Marley was great."

Marley had a very good time with the people in the film company. Everybody played with him and petted him.

After four days, the cameramen stopped filming.

"Call us after eight months," said Bob Gosse. "The movie will be ready then."

After eight months, we called the company. The name of the movie was *The Last Home Run*, but we couldn't learn anything about it. I called the company again and again.

Two years later, I was in a store and there were a lot of movies on the shelves. Suddenly, I saw *The Last Home Run*. Marley's movie! I bought it and took it home.

"Come and watch this!" I shouted to Jenny and the children.

We saw Marley in the movie. He was only there for two minutes, but it was very exciting. We all laughed and cried.

"We're famous!" shouted Patrick.

Marley's name came at the end of the film. In big letters, it said, "Marley the Dog."

♦

Some time later, we said goodbye to our home in West Palm Beach. The place got more and more dangerous, and our house was too small for two children and a large dog. So we moved to a bigger house in another city, Boca Raton. A lot of rich people lived in Boca Raton. They had expensive cars, big houses, and beautiful clothes.

There were many good things about our new house. Near the house was a small park. But, best of all, it had a pool. We all loved the pool, but Marley loved it most. He jumped in with me and climbed on me.

But there was a problem with the garage in our new house. It had no windows and it got very hot in summer. So we couldn't put Marley in it when there was a thunderstorm.

I took Patrick and Conor to the pet store and we bought a strong cage for Marley. We put it next to the washing machine.

I put some food in the cage. "Come here, Marley," I called. Marley went inside and I closed the door of the cage after him.

Marley loved to swim in the pool.

He lay down on the floor and chewed his food happily.

"This is going to be your new home when we're away," I said.

That evening, we went out for dinner. Before we left, I opened the door of the cage. Marley walked inside and I closed the door.

"Be a good boy, Marley," I said.

We had dinner in a restaurant, then we went for a walk.

"This is great," said Jenny. "We can forget about Marley. We know he's fine in the cage." She smiled happily.

We went home and walked to the front door. I looked at the window next to it. Something was there, in the window— something black, and wet. It was Marley's nose.

"What's that?" I said. "How could ... Marley?"

24

When I opened the front door, Marley ran to us happily. Everything in the house was fine. Then we looked at the cage. The door was open.

"But how did Marley get out?" asked Jenny.

"He opened the door from inside," I said. "He's smart, and he's very strong."

Day after day, when we left the house, we put Marley into the cage. When we came home, sometimes he was there. Sometimes he was at the window. We tried to make the cage stronger, but Marley was stronger than the cage. When he wanted to get out, he pushed the door open.

Chapter 7 The World's Worst Dog

Many people in Boca Raton had dogs, but their dogs were very different from Marley. Most of these dogs were very, very small. Rich women carried them in their handbags, and took them into expensive stores, and in their fast cars. Marley wanted very much to be friends with these small dogs, but the dogs didn't want to be friends with Marley.

The weather in Boca Raton was very good, so lots of restaurants had tables and chairs outside. Customers brought their dogs with them to the restaurants. People ate their food or drank coffee, and their dogs lay quietly on the ground.

One Sunday afternoon, we went out for lunch. We parked our car and walked up and down the street. Many other people were out with their dogs, too. Marley walked next to me on his leash.

We found a restaurant and sat down outside. I put Marley's leash around one of the legs of the strong, heavy table. The waiter came and we asked for some drinks. Then Jenny held up her glass happily.

"To a beautiful day with my beautiful family!" she said.

Suddenly, our table started to move. It moved quickly between the other tables and the other customers.

"What's happening?" I thought. Then I saw a small white dog across the street. "Marley's going to that dog," I shouted. "We have to stop him!"

We jumped up and ran after Marley and the table.

"Sorry! Sorry! Sorry!" we shouted to the other customers.

I ran and grabbed the table. Jenny grabbed it, too. We held it and it stopped moving. I turned around and saw the faces of the other customers. Everybody looked at us with their mouths open.

We carried the table back to its place, and a waiter came.

"I'll get some more drinks for you," he said.

"No," said Jenny. "We'll pay for our drinks and leave."

♦

Jenny and I had another baby. This time it was a girl and we named her Colleen.

When Colleen was two months old, I had my fortieth birthday. I wanted to do something exciting on my birthday, but it was a very quiet day. When I arrived home from work, Jenny was tired. By eight-thirty, all three children were asleep and Jenny was, too.

I felt a little sad. I took a drink outside. I sat and looked at the ocean. Marley lay on the ground next to me. I thought about my life, then I thought about Marley. He wasn't a puppy now; he was six years old. But he loved life and he was very happy.

"Marley," I said, "it's only you and me tonight." I held up my glass. "We're not young, but we're having a good time."

Some days later, my friend Jim called me.

"Let's go out for a drink on Saturday," he said.

Jim came for me at six o'clock and we went out to a bar. We talked and laughed. Then the barman called out, "Is John

Grogan here? There's a phone call for John Grogan."

It was Jenny. "The baby's crying," she said. "Can you come and help me?"

"I'll take you home," Jim said.

When we turned into my street, I saw a lot of cars.

"Somebody's having a party," I said.

Jim stopped the car outside my house and I invited him inside. Then, suddenly, the front door opened. Jenny stood there with Colleen in her arms. She had a big smile on her face.

I looked into the yard. There were lots of people around the pool—my friends and neighbors.

"HAPPY BIRTHDAY, JOHN!" they shouted.

♦

I wanted to take Marley to the beach. You couldn't take pets onto most beaches in South Florida, but one small beach was different. Everybody called it Dog Beach. On Dog Beach, dogs could run freely. They didn't have to be on a leash.

One morning in June, I took Marley to Dog Beach. There were lots of people with dogs, but the dogs were on leashes.

"What happened?" I asked a man.

"The police came," the man said. "We have to use a leash."

So I walked Marley on his leash. But I felt sorry for him.

After our walk, I gave Marley a bowl of water. Then a man arrived with a big black dog. It looked dangerous.

"Don't be afraid of him," said the man. "This is Killer. But he's very friendly. He doesn't fight other dogs."

I told the man about the police.

"That's stupid!" he shouted. "This is Dog Beach!"

He took off Killer's leash, and Killer ran into the water. Marley looked at Killer and then he looked at me. I could read his thoughts: *Please! Please! Please! I'll be good!*

I looked around the beach. I couldn't see any policemen.

I took off Marley's leash and he ran into the ocean after Killer. Marley and Killer played happily in the water. Other people watched them. Then they took off their dogs' leashes, too. The dogs ran into the water.

But then Marley started to drink from the ocean.

"Stop that, Marley!" I cried. "You'll be sick!"

But Marley didn't listen to me and he didn't stop drinking. Then he started to turn around in the water.

"Oh, no!" I thought. I ran into the water.

But it was too late. Marley pooped everywhere.

"Hey!" somebody shouted angrily. "Get your dog!"

"Marley, no!" I shouted. I could feel everybody's eyes on me—and on Marley. "No, Marley, no! No! No! No!"

Marley's poop was everywhere. The other people grabbed their dogs. Marley came out of the dirty water and looked at me happily. But we had to leave.

Marley drank a lot of water from the ocean.

"That wasn't nice," the man with Killer said.

"Sorry," I said. I put Marley's leash on him.

Other dogs didn't drink water from the ocean. Marley wasn't a bad dog, but sometimes he did stupid things.

"What's wrong with you, Marley?" I said on the drive home. "Sometimes you're the worst dog in the world."

I never took Marley to the beach again.

Chapter 8 We Move North

When Colleen was two years old, I got a job with a magazine in Pennsylvania, in the north-east of the United States.

We were ready for a change from Florida. There were too many people and cars. The weather was always hot, with a lot of thunderstorms. We wanted to live in a quiet place in the country. We wanted to see summer, winter, spring, and fall. Most of all, we wanted to see snow.

Our new home was very beautiful. There was a small river near our house and there were woods all around it. Marley was very happy. He loved playing in the woods, and running after small animals.

Three weeks after New Year, it snowed. The children were very excited because it was their first time. We put on warm jackets and ran outside. Marley followed us.

Marley was very funny in the snow. He fell down all the time. Snow lay on his fur and his face. I could only see a black nose and two brown eyes. I could read his thoughts:

I don't understand. What's this? It feels so cold and wet.

But then Marley jumped up again. He ran around the yard and jumped through the snow. The children laughed happily, and Marley was happy, too. We had a great time.

♦

It was almost the end of our first winter in Pennsylvania. We were very happy in our new house.

But Marley was nine years old now. He moved more slowly and he slept for most of the day. Sometimes when I took him for a walk, he got very tired. His fur in many places was gray, not yellow.

Life with Marley wasn't easy. He cost us a lot of money. He ate a lot of food and he broke a lot of our things. We could never change him. We knew that. But he was one of our family. He loved us and we loved him.

That spring, I said to Jenny, "Let's get some farm animals."

"OK," she said. "But we don't have a place for big animals. Let's get some chickens. Then we can have eggs every day."

Jenny talked to one of the moms at the children's school. Donna lived on a farm. She gave Jenny four baby chickens.

The chickens lived in a box in the kitchen. They ate and pooped. Then they ate some more—and they got bigger.

One morning, I woke up early when I heard a call from downstairs: *Cock-a-doodle-do!*

I woke Jenny up and asked, "What's that noise?"

"Oh," she said. "I don't know." She turned over and slept.

Every morning, the chickens made a lot of noise. Sometimes they made loud noises very near Marley. Marley was usually afraid of loud noises, but he didn't move away from the chickens.

"That's strange," I thought. "Can't Marley hear the chickens?"

One afternoon when Marley was asleep in the kitchen, I walked up behind him.

"Marley!" I said. But Marley didn't move. "Marley!" I said again. Nothing. "MARLEY!" I shouted. Marley turned. He stood up and wagged his tail.

"Oh, no," I thought. "Marley can't hear."

But Marley *could* hear some things. When we put food in his bowl, he always heard the sound of his dinner. He ran in from the next room.

Marley was always hungry. He ate four big bowls of dog food every day, and he also ate our food. Labradors are big dogs, and Marley was a very large Labrador. But he never got fat.

One day I came home from work early and I went into the kitchen. Marley was there. He didn't see me and he didn't hear me. There was a sandwich on the kitchen table. Marley stood up and put his paws on the table. Then he ate the sandwich.

"What are you doing, Marley?" I asked. "You are a bad dog." But he didn't hear me. He ate the sandwich happily.

I put my hand on Marley's fur and he jumped. When he saw me, he lay down on the floor. He looked up at me and I started to laugh. I couldn't be angry with Marley. He was old now and he couldn't hear. I couldn't change him.

The chickens weren't afraid of Marley and he never tried to catch them. They walked around the yard and Marley went with them.

Chapter 9 Marley Gets Older

Jenny and I had a good life. Our children were young. We felt young, too. But when we looked at Marley, we saw many changes. The years went past, and he was twelve years old. By this time, he couldn't hear anything. His fur was gray. His teeth were brown.

Late one night, I took Marley outside for his walk before bed. It was winter and there was a cold rain. I went back into the house for my jacket. When I came out again, Marley wasn't there. I looked for him everywhere, but I couldn't find him.

I went back inside. Then I walked upstairs and woke up Jenny.

"I can't find Marley," I said. "He's out there in the rain."

Jenny pulled on her jeans and shoes and we went outside again. I walked slowly through the woods and called for Marley. Jenny went a different way. We were very wet and cold.

"Let's go home and get warm," I said. "I'll get the car and come out again."

We walked back to our house. Suddenly, we saw Marley. He stood outside the house, out of the rain. When he saw us, he was very happy. I felt angry with him, but then I was happy, too.

I brought him inside and dried him. Marley was very tired. He went to sleep and woke up at noon the next day.

♦

Marley couldn't see well now. His fur started to fall out, too. Jenny cleaned the house every day, but his hairs were everywhere. But Marley's biggest problem was his hips. They hurt him a lot and he couldn't move quickly. He couldn't climb the stairs easily. But he tried to follow us everywhere.

Marley had good days and bad days. One spring evening, I took him for a short walk around the yard. The night was cold and there was a light wind. I ran and Marley ran with me.

"Marley!" I said. "You're a puppy again!"

We ran back to the house. There were two small stairs in front of the door. When Marley tried to climb the stairs, he fell down. He lay on the stairs and looked sadly up at me.

Marley was too heavy for me. I couldn't carry him, so I had to push him up the stairs. Then he stood up and went into the house.

When I looked at Marley, I thought, "We only have one life and it can change very quickly."

I enjoyed my job on the magazine, but I really wanted to work for a newspaper again. Newspapers were more exciting, and I liked writing about big stories. I also liked getting letters and calls from readers.

A friend told me about a job on the *Philadelphia Inquirer*. This was one of the best newspapers in the United States. I wrote to the newspaper and I got the job. I was very happy.

♦

In the summer, Jenny visited her sister in Boston. She took the children with her. I didn't go because I was busy with my new job. Every day, I was away from home for ten or twelve hours, so we took Marley to a vacation home for dogs.

Some days later, an animal doctor called me from the home.

"I'm sorry," she said, "but Marley's very sick. When he saw the other dogs, he got very excited. He ate his food too quickly. Then he had a bad problem with his stomach and he almost died. He's a little better now, but it will happen again."

"Oh," I said. "What are you saying?"

"Do you want us to help end Marley's life?" she said. "I'm sorry."

"Oh," I said. I couldn't think. "I have to talk to my wife."

I called Jenny in Boston and we had a long conversation about Marley. In the end, Jenny said, "The doctor's right. We have to do the best thing for Marley."

I called the doctor back. "Yes, Marley's a very old dog," I said. "Life isn't so good for him now. He doesn't have many teeth and he can't hear. His hips hurt him, too."

"Yes," she said. "Maybe we have to put him to sleep. But I'll call you again in an hour."

When the doctor called again, she said, "Marley's a very sick dog, but he isn't getting worse."

The next morning, she called again. "We can wait," she said. "Marley's eating. You can take him home tomorrow."

I was very happy. The next evening, after work, I went to

the dogs' home. Marley was very thin and weak. I thanked the doctor.

"Everybody here loves Marley," she said.

One of the workers helped me put Marley into the car. Then I drove him home. He couldn't climb the stairs to the bedroom and I didn't want to leave him. So, that night, I put a sleeping bag on the floor and lay down next to him.

"Tomorrow Jenny and the children are coming back," I said. "But tonight, Marley, it's only you and me."

I thought about my first night with Marley, when he was a small puppy. That night, he cried for his mother, and then he slept in a box next to my bed. Now, thirteen years later, here we were again. I put out my hand and petted him.

♦

In the next weeks, Marley got a little better. A lot of the time, he lay on the floor in the family room, asleep in the sun.

But one morning, when I was in the bedroom, I heard a noise. Then Conor shouted, "Help! Marley fell down the stairs!"

Marley lay at the bottom of the stairs. Jenny and I ran to him. But then he got up and walked away.

"Marley had a bad fall," I told the children. "But he's OK."

But Marley was hurt. When I got home from work that evening, he couldn't move. When he saw me, he tried to get up. But he fell down again on the floor.

"I don't think Marley can go upstairs again," I said.

But I was wrong. The next day, I was upstairs at my computer in my bedroom when I heard a sound. I turned around. Marley stood at the bedroom door!

"Marley!" I said. "What are you doing here?"

I went to him and petted him. Then I looked into his eyes.

"Marley," I said, "you're going to tell me when it's time—right?"

Chapter 10 A Great Dog

Winter arrived early that year. The children waited for the snow.

"Can Marley live through another winter?" I thought.

Jenny and I took the children to Disney World in Florida. It was their first Christmas away from home and they were very excited. Jenny took Marley to the animal doctors' office. They gave him a home there and watched him carefully.

We had a great family vacation. But on the way home, somebody called us from the doctors' office.

"Marley's very tired," she said, "and his hips are really hurting him."

The next day, Jenny went for Marley. He got out of the car, but he couldn't walk into the house. He lay on the ground outside. Jenny called me at work.

"I can't get Marley inside," she said. "He can't get up."

I left my office and went home. When I arrived, Marley was inside the house. But he was very sick. He lay on the floor. For the first time in thirteen years, he didn't get up when he saw me. His eyes followed me, but he didn't move his head. I looked at his stomach; it was very big.

I called the animal doctors.

"Bring Marley here now," a young woman doctor said.

I looked at Jenny and she looked at me.

"Marley has to go to the hospital," we told the children. "The doctors are going to try to make him better. But he's very sick."

With Jenny's help, I put Marley into the back of the car. He lay on the floor. I petted his head.

"Oh, Marley," I said again and again.

At the hospital, I helped him out of the car and took him inside. The young doctor took him away. Then she came back and showed me some pictures of the inside of Marley's stomach.

"I'm very sorry," she said quietly. "We can't do anything for Marley now."

"I understand," I said. "Please can I say goodbye to him?"

"Yes, of course," she said. "Have as much time with him as you want."

Marley was asleep. I got down next to him and ran my fingers through his fur. I held up each ear in my hands. I opened his mouth and looked at his teeth. Then I held up his front paw.

"I want you to understand something, Marley," I said. "Sometimes we called you the world's worst dog. But you're not. We never told you this before … but you're a great dog, Marley. A *great* dog."

I sat with Marley for a long time, then I called the doctor.

"I'm ready now," I said.

I held Marley's head and the doctor gave Marley something. It didn't hurt him. He died quietly.

"I want to take Marley home," I said.

Two people brought a large black bag out to my car. Then I thanked the doctor and drove away. When I got home, the children were in bed. I put my arms around Jenny and we cried for a long time.

Later, we went outside. We took the black bag out of the car and put it into the garage.

Next morning, Jenny told the children about Marley. They were very sad and started to cry.

"It's OK," I said. "When you have a dog, this always happens. Dogs don't live as long as people."

Conor made a picture and wrote a letter for Marley:

To Marley. I loved you all my life. You were always there when I wanted you. Your brother, Conor Richard Grogan.

Colleen made a picture of a girl with a big yellow dog. She wrote under the picture: *I will never forget you, Marley.*

I found a very good place for Marley, in the ground under two big fruit trees. I put the black bag in the ground, and Jenny and the children watched. After I finished, everybody said, "We love you, Marley."

Then we went back to the kitchen and told stories about Marley. Sometimes we laughed and sometimes we cried.

The next days were very difficult. The house was very quiet. When I came home at night, there was no Marley. Jenny cleaned the house, but his fur was everywhere. One morning, when I put on my shoes, I found some of Marley's fur inside them.

Marley was my dog for thirteen years. He wasn't an obedient dog, but he was important in my life. I wanted to tell other people about him. So I wrote about him in my newspaper.

Nobody called Marley a great dog … or a good dog, I wrote. He was wild and crazy. He had to leave obedience school. He chewed things, and he wasn't very intelligent. But he understood people's feelings, and he was very good with children.

A person can learn a lot from a dog. Because of him, I listened to my feelings. Because of him, I enjoyed winter sunlight and the snow and a walk in the woods. Because of him, I can be a good friend.

A dog can show us the important things in life. A dog isn't interested in fast cars or big houses or expensive clothes. Give a dog your love, and he will give you his.

◆

Many people read about Marley in the newspaper. Animal lovers called me and wrote to me. They wrote to me about their love for dogs. They wrote about their feelings when their dogs died.

Many people wrote funny stories about their dogs. Some people wrote, "Marley wasn't the worst dog in the world. *My* dog's the worst dog in the world!" I began to feel better.

I took the letters home and showed them to Jenny. She

laughed, too.

Winter came to an end and it was spring. Our yard was full of flowers. I didn't think about Marley all the time. When I thought about him, I usually remembered the happy days.

In many ways, life without a dog was easier. The house and the yard were clean. We could enjoy going out to dinner. But something about our family wasn't right.

One morning, Jenny showed me the newspaper.

"Look at this," she said.

It was an ad for a dog. I saw a photo of a big yellow Labrador. I looked at the photo, then I looked again.

"That's Marley!" I said.

"It isn't Marley," said Jenny. "Look."

Under the photo was the dog's name: Lucky. I read:

I'm looking for a new home and a new family. I want a quiet home, because I'm a little wild.

We read the ad and looked at the photo again. We didn't say anything for some time.

Then I said, "We can go and *look* at him."

"Yes," said Jenny. "Why not?"

ACTIVITIES

Chapters 1–2

Before you read

1 Does your family have a pet? Talk about your pet, or about a friend's pet.
   a What is it?
   b What is its name?
   c How did you (or your friend) get it?
   d What does it eat?
   e What does it like to do?
   f What does it not like to do?

2 Do you like dogs? Why (not)? Do many people in your country have dogs in their homes?

3 Look at the Word List at the back of the book.
   a Which are words for:
      1) a young dog?
      2) a kind of weather?
      3) a very, very small animal?
   b Why:
      1) do dogs wag their tails?
      2) do people read newspaper ads?
      3) do people have plants in their houses?

While you read

4 What happened first? And then? Number these sentences 1–7.
   a The plant died.   ......
   b John moved to Florida and married Jenny.   ......
   c John and Jenny went to see some puppies.   ......
   d John's father gave him a dog.   ......
   e Jenny saw an ad in the newspaper.   ......
   f John bought a plant for Jenny.   ......
   g A large yellow dog ran out of the woods.   ......

After you read

5 Why are these important in the story?

a   Bob Marley
b   Buddy, a dog
c   strong chemicals

6   Look at the picture of Marley on page 5. What other words
can you write around the picture? (head, eyes …)

Chapters 3–4

Before you read

7   Talk about these questions with a friend.
a   Why do people have pets?
b   What problems can there be with pets?
c   What can dogs learn in an obedience class?
d   What can people do with their pets when they go on
vacation?

While you read

8   Finish the sentences with the words on the right.
a   Dr. Jay   grabbed things and chewed them.
b   John   often has bad thunderstorms.
c   The teacher   gave Jenny a beautiful chain.
d   Kathy   has small country roads.
e   Patrick   understood dogs very well.
f   Ireland   stayed in John and Jenny's home.
g   Florida   was Marley's new best friend.
h   Marley   didn't want Marley in the obedience
                     class.

After you read

9   Work with another student. Student A is John Grogan,
and Student B is Dr. Jay. Talk about Marley's problems in
thunderstorms. Begin the conversation in this way:
Student A: Hello, Dr. Jay. Can I talk to you about Marley?
Student B: Yes, of course. How can I help you?
*Student A: Well, Marley is afraid of thunder. He has bad
problems in thunderstorms.*
Student B: Really? What does he do?

Chapters 5–6

Before you read

10 Do you like movies about animals? Why (not)? Think of a movie about an animal and tell a friend the story.

   a What kind of animal was in the story?

   b What happened in the story?

   c What happened to the animal at the end?

While you read

11 Read the sentences. How do they end? Underline the right words.

   a One night, John heard a cry in the street. It was …
      a small child.   a young man.   a girl.

   b When Jenny was in hospital, John did the housework …
      very well.   but not very well.   very badly.

   c When Conor was born, Patrick was …
      twelve months old.   seventeen months old.
      two years old.

   d When Conor was a small baby, Jenny wanted …
      Marley to leave.   Marley to stay.   to get a new dog.

   e A lot of newspaper ads were from people with …
      dogs' homes.   Labrador puppies.   Labrador dogs.

   f Marley's second time at the obedience class was …
      better.   worse.   the same.

After you read

12 Answer these questions.

   a Who was Bob Gosse? Why was he interested in Marley?

   b How did John find out about Marley's movie?

   c Why did the Grogan family move from West Palm Beach?

   d What did they like best about their new house?

   e What was the problem with Marley's cage?

Chapters 7–8

Before you read

13 What did the Grogans like about Marley? What did they not like about him? Would you like Marley in your home?

14 Before you get a dog, what do you have to think about? Talk about these ideas with a friend. Then think of other ideas and discuss them.
- the cost of dog food
- walking the dog
- cleaning the dog

While you read

15 Are these sentences right (✓) or wrong (✗)?

  a Most dogs in Boca Raton were very large. ......

  b Marley pulled a table away from a restaurant. ......

  c John had a party on his fortieth birthday. ......

  d You could take dogs to most beaches in South Florida. ......

  e Marley pooped in the ocean at Dog Beach. ......

  f John got a job with a newspaper a long way from Florida. ......

  g At their new home, Marley could not see the chickens very well. ......

After you read

16 Which person or animal had these thoughts?

  a "Why don't these dogs want to be friends with me?"

  b "It's my birthday today. I really want to do something exciting, but Jenny's too tired."

  c "I'm going to invite our friends to a party for John. But I'm not going to tell him about it."

  d "I can never take Marley to Dog Beach again."

  e "That sandwich looks good. Nobody's here. I'm going to eat it!"

Chapters 9–10

Before you read

17 Discuss these questions with a friend.

  a How does a dog change when it gets old?

  b What can people do for sick animals?

  c Are there places for sick animals in your country?

18 There are mistakes in these sentences. Cross out the mistakes and write the right words.

    a When Marley got old, his fur was yellow. ....

    b John started work at another magazine. ....

    c When Jenny went to Boston, Marley stayed with John. ....

    d After Marley died, John and Jenny saw an ad for a different kind of dog. ....

After you read

19 Work with another student. Student A is John, and Student B is Jenny. When Jenny was in Florida, John called her about Marley. Have their conversation. Begin in this way:

    Student A: *Hello, Jenny. I'm sorry, but I have to tell you something. Marley's very sick.*

    Student B: *Oh, no! What happened?*

20 Discuss these questions with a friend.

    a "Marley," I said, "you're going to tell me when it's time—right?" What did John mean? Why did he say that?

    b "A person can learn a lot from a dog." What did John mean? What other ideas do you have?

    c How did people's letters about their dogs help John and Jenny?

    d Do you think Marley really was "the world's worst dog"?

Writing

21 Write about Marley. In what ways was he a bad pet? In what ways was he a good pet? Why were the Grogans very sad when he died?

22 You have some puppies and you want to sell them. Write a newspaper ad.

23 You are John. Your oldest son, Patrick, is asking you about your first dog, Shaun. Write the conversation.

24 You work for a vacation company in Ireland. Write an ad for a vacation with your company.

25 You are John. Write some notes for Kathy about Marley.

Food:

Water:

Fleas:

Walks:

Thunderstorms:

26 You work for a newspaper in Florida. Write a story about Lisa, John's seventeen-year-old neighbor.

27 Write a letter to John Grogan at the end of the story. Tell him about your dog, or another animal.

28 Tell the story of a book or a movie about an animal.